# PR
# YOUR HEART

# PREPARE YOUR HEART

## DAILY ADVENT REFLECTIONS
### FROM
# POPE FRANCIS

Edited by Theresa Khoo and
Marianne Lorraine Trouvé, FSP

BOOKS & MEDIA

Boston

Library of Congress Cataloging-in-Publication Data

Names: Francis, Pope, 1936- author.

Title: Prepare your heart : daily Advent reflections with Pope Francis / edited by Theresa Khoo and Marianne Lorraine.

Description: Boston, MA : Pauline Books & Media, 2018.

Identifiers: LCCN 2018004920| ISBN 9780819860477 (pbk.) | ISBN 0819860476 (pbk.)

Subjects: LCSH: Advent--Prayers and devotions. | Catholic Church--Prayers and devotions.

Classification: LCC BV40 .F7313 2018 | DDC 242/.332--dc23

LC record available at https://lccn.loc.gov/2018004920

Excerpts from Pope Francis's audiences, homilies, angelus messages, addresses, messages and exhortations copyright © Libreria Editrice Vaticana. Used with permission.

Prayers written by Marianne Lorraine Trouvé, FSP; reflection questions written by Theresa Khoo.

Unless otherwise noted, the Scripture quotations contained in the excerpts are taken directly from Pope Francis's works.

All other Scripture quotations contained herein are from the *New Revised Standard Version Bible: Catholic Edition,* copyright © 1989, 1993, Division of Christian Education of the National Council of the Churches of Christ in the United States of America. Used by permission. All rights reserved.

Cover design by Rosana Usselmann

Cover photo: istockphoto / © Romolo Tavani

"P" and PAULINE are registered trademarks of the Daughters of St. Paul.

Published by Pauline Books & Media, 50 Saint Paul's Avenue, Boston, MA 02130–3491

Printed in the U.S.A.

www.pauline.org

Pauline Books & Media is the publishing house of the Daughters of St. Paul, an international congregation of women religious serving the Church with the communications media.

1 2 3 4 5 6 7 8 9                                    22 21 20 19 18

# Contents

# WEEK 1

# *Opening Our Hearts to God*

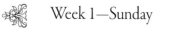 

# Keep Watch

"Therefore keep watch, because you do not know on what day your Lord will come. . . . So you also must be ready, because the Son of Man will come at an hour when you do not expect him."

—Matthew 24:42–44

[This] passage of the Gospel (cf. Mt 24:37–44) introduces us to one of the most evocative themes of Advent: *the visit of the Lord to humanity.* . . .

The Word of God emphasizes the contrast between the normal unfolding of events, the everyday *routine,* and the unexpected coming of the Lord. . . . It always strikes a chord when we think about the hours which precede a great disaster: everyone is calm, and they go about their usual business without realizing that their lives are about to be turned upside down. Of course, the Gospel does not want to scare us, but to open our horizons to *another*, greater dimension, one which, on the one hand, puts into perspective everyday things, while at the same time making them precious, crucial. The relationship with the God-who-comes-to-visit-us gives every gesture, every thing, a different light, a substance, a symbolic value.

*Angelus, November 27, 2016*

## REFLECTION

How am I awake or asleep to the events happening in my life?

## PRAYER

Jesus, help me to be alert so that I won't miss the signs of your presence in my life.

## Stay Vigilant

But understand this: If the owner of the house had known at what time of night the thief was coming, he would have kept watch and would not have let his house be broken into.

—Matthew 24:43

There also comes an invitation to *sobriety*, to not be controlled by the things of this world, by material reality, but rather to govern them. If, by contrast, we allow ourselves to be influenced and overpowered by these things, we cannot perceive that there is something very important: our final encounter with the Lord. . . . And everyday matters must have this horizon, and must be directed to that horizon—this encounter with the Lord who comes for us. In that moment, as the Gospel says, "Then two men will be in the field; one is taken and one is left" (Mt 24:40). It is an invitation to be vigilant, because in not knowing when he will come, we need to be ever ready to leave.

*Angelus, November 27, 2016*

## REFLECTION

What am I watchful and waiting for right now?

## PRAYER

Sometimes, Lord, my life seems so ordinary. But I believe that you are at work even in the small things that happen each day. Open my eyes that I may see your gentle, loving Providence that guides me to you.

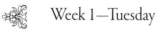 

## Week 1—Tuesday

# Let God Change Your Life

By the tender mercy of our God,
    the dawn from on high will break upon us.

—Luke 1:78

In [the] season of Advent, we are called to expand the horizons of our hearts, to be amazed by the life which presents itself each day with newness. In order to do this, we must learn to not depend on our own certainties, on our own established strategies, because the Lord comes at a time that we do not imagine. He comes to bring us into a more beautiful and grand dimension.

May Our Lady, the Virgin of Advent, help us not to consider ourselves proprietors of our life, not to resist when the Lord comes to change it, but to be ready to let ourselves be visited by him, the awaited and welcome guest, even if it disturbs our plans.

*Angelus, November 27, 2016*

## REFLECTION

How do I deal with surprises or setbacks in my life?

## PRAYER

Teach me, Lord, to turn to you with trust each day.

# Find God in Humility

But you, O Bethlehem of Ephrathah,
    who are one of the little clans of Judah,
from you shall come forth for me
    one who is to rule in Israel.

—Micah 5:2

God comes to save us. He finds no better way to do so than to walk with us, living our life. . . . [H]e didn't choose a great city of a great empire; he did not choose a princess or a countess for his Mother, an important person; he didn't choose a luxurious palace. It seems as if everything was intentionally done in near obscurity. Mary was a girl of sixteen or seventeen . . . in a faraway village on the outskirts of the Roman Empire. . . . Joseph was a youth who loved her and wanted to marry her. He was a carpenter who earned his daily bread. All in simplicity, all in obscurity.... All was hidden, all was humble. The great cities of the world knew nothing about it....

This is how God is among us. If you want to find God, seek him in humility, seek him in poverty, seek him where he is hidden: in the neediest, in the sick, in the hungry, in the imprisoned.

*Homily, December 18, 2015*

## REFLECTION

What are my attitudes toward the poor, the marginalized and those different from me?

## PRAYER

Jesus, you turned our human way of looking at things upside down. In your eyes power and wealth count for nothing, but humility and love are the precious gems of your kingdom. I want to live according to your standards.

# Let God's Mercy Embrace You

Open the gates,
   so that the righteous nation that keeps faith
   may enter in.

—Isaiah 26:2

[Jesus] will not say to you: come with me because you made so many fine offerings to the Church, you are a benefactor of the Church, come, come to heaven. No. The entrance to heaven is not bought with money. He will not say: you are very important. You have studied so much and received so many honors. Come to heaven. No. Honors do not open the doors to heaven.

What will Jesus say to open the doors of heaven to us? "I was hungry and you gave me to eat; I was homeless and you gave me a home; I was sick and you visited me; I was in prison and you came to me" (cf. Mt 25:35–36). Jesus exists in humility. . . . But Jesus says more: if the greatest sinners repent, they will go before us to heaven. They have the key. Those who give alms and those who let themselves be embraced by the Lord's mercy.

*Homily, December 18, 2015*


## REFLECTION

Am I willing to humble myself and tell Jesus that I need his mercy?


## PRAYER

I want to go to heaven and be with you forever, Jesus. Teach me how to live so that when the end of my life comes, I will be ready to meet you.

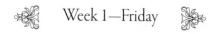
# Seek Jesus in Those in Need

Listen! I am standing at the door, knocking; if you hear my voice and open the door, I will come in to you and eat with you, and you with me.

—Revelation 3:20

Today . . . we ask for two things. First: that the Lord open the door of our heart, of everyone. We are all in need. We are all sinners. We all need to hear the Lord's word and need the Lord's Word to come. Second: that the Lord make us understand that the way of presumption, the way of wealth, the way of vanity, the way of pride is not the way to salvation. May the Lord make us understand that his fatherly caress, his mercy, his for-giveness is when we approach those who suffer, those discarded by society: Jesus is there. . . . He alone gives us mercy and grace. And to receive this grace we must approach those who have been discarded, the poor, those in great need, because we will all be judged on how we draw close to them.

. . . God is wounded by love, and this why he can save us all. May the Lord give us this grace.

*Homily, December 18, 2015*

## REFLECTION

Am I ready to open my heart to everyone so as to receive God's grace and love?

## PRAYER

I want to dine with you, Jesus, at the banquet of eternal life. And I want to bring others to you as well. Sustain us on our journey to the heavenly kingdom.

# Be Merciful Like the Father

[The LORD] heals the brokenhearted,
   and binds up their wounds.

—Psalm 147:3

Today too, Jesus lives and walks along the paths of
ordinary life in order to draw near to everyone,
beginning with the least, and to heal us of our infirmities
and illnesses. . . . I invite you to listen to and follow Jesus,
and to allow yourselves to be transformed interiorly by
his words, which "are spirit and life" (Jn 6:62). . . . Let us
dispose our hearts therefore to being "good soil," by lis-
tening, receiving and living out the word, and thus
bearing fruit. The more we unite ourselves to Jesus

through prayer, Sacred Scripture, the Eucharist, the sacraments celebrated and lived in the Church and in fraternity, the more there will grow in us the joy of cooperating with God in the service of the Kingdom of mercy and truth, of justice and peace. And the harvest will be plentiful, proportionate to the grace we have meekly welcomed into our lives.

*Message for the 51st World Day*
*of Prayer for Vocations, May 11, 2014*

## Reflection

How does God want me to love in a radical way?

## Prayer

I thank you, Lord, for looking on me with love. Grant that I may know how to give that love to others.

# The Immaculate Conception of Mary

Blessed be the God and Father of our Lord Jesus Christ, who has blessed us in Christ with every spiritual blessing in the heavenly places.

—Ephesians 1:3

The feast of the Immaculate Conception expresses the grandeur of God's love. Not only does he forgive sin, but in Mary he even averts the original sin present in every man and woman who comes into this world. This is *the love of God which precedes, anticipates and saves.* The beginning of the history of sin in the Garden of Eden yields to a plan of saving love. The words of Genesis reflect our own daily experience: we are constantly tempted to disobedience, a disobedience expressed in wanting to go about our lives without regard for God's will. This is the enmity which keeps striking at people's lives, setting them in opposition to God's plan. Yet the history of sin can only be understood in the light of God's love and forgiveness. Sin can only be understood in this light. Were sin the only thing that mattered, we would be the most desperate of creatures. But the promised triumph of Christ's love enfolds everything in the Father's mercy. The word of God which we have just heard leaves no doubt about this. The Immaculate Virgin stands before us as a privileged witness of this promise and its fulfillment.

*Homily December 8, 2015*

## REFLECTION

Can I remember a recent experience of God's love and forgiveness, and thank God for it?

## PRAYER

Mary Immaculate, God chose you to be the mother of Jesus, his Son. You accepted this mission with love. Pray for me that I may fulfill my daily duties with love for God and for those whom I can serve.

## WEEK 2

# *John the Baptist and the Deserts of Humanity*

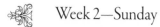 
# The Necessity of Conversion

"Live by the Spirit, I say, and do not gratify the desires of the flesh."

—Galatians 5:16

On this second Sunday of Advent, the Liturgy places us in the school of John the Baptist, who preached "a baptism of repentance for the forgiveness of sins." Perhaps we ask ourselves, "Why do we have to convert? Conversion is about an atheist who becomes a believer or a sinner who becomes just. But we don't need it. We are already Christians. So we are okay." . . . It is precisely because of this presumption . . . that we must convert: from the supposition that, all things considered, things are fine as they are and we don't need any kind of conversion. . . . Let us ask ourselves: is it true that . . . we have within us the same feelings that Jesus has? Is it true that we feel as Christ feels? For example, when we suffer some wrongdoing or some insult, do we manage to react without animosity and to forgive from the heart those who apologize to us? . . . We can ask ourselves so many questions. . . . We must always convert and have the sentiments that Jesus had.

*Angelus, December 6, 2015*

## REFLECTION

How can I live in a constant state of *metanoia*—of converting and changing my way of life?

## PRAYER

Lord, help me to look into my heart and see those places where I need a conversion. Give me the grace and courage to make any necessary changes.

# Accepting Salvation

A voice cries out:
"In the wilderness prepare the way of the LORD,
  make straight in the desert a highway for our God.

—Isaiah 40:3

The voice of the Baptist still cries in the deserts of humanity today, which are . . . closed minds and hardened hearts. And [his voice] causes us to ask ourselves if we are actually following the right path, living a life according to the Gospel. Today, as then, he admonishes us with the words of the Prophet Isaiah: "Prepare the way of the Lord!" (v. 4) It is a pressing invitation to open one's heart and receive the salvation that God offers ceaselessly, almost obstinately, because he wants us all to be free from the slavery of sin. But the text of the prophet amplifies this voice, portending that "all flesh shall see the salvation of God" (v. 6). And salvation is offered to every man, and every people, without exclusion, to each one of us. None of us can say, "I'm a saint; I'm perfect; I'm already saved." No. We must always accept this offer of salvation.

*Angelus, December 6, 2015*

## REFLECTION

God's invitation of salvation is for me. Where in my life do I need Jesus to come and save me?

## PRAYER

Jesus, send me your Holy Spirit to enlighten my mind and heart. Show me those places in my life where I can make more room for you.

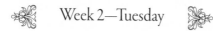 

# Make Straight the Path to God

It is no longer I who live, but it is Christ who lives in me. And the life I now live in the flesh I live by faith in the Son of God, who loved me and gave himself for me.

—Galatians 2:20

If our Lord Jesus has changed our lives . . . how can we not feel the passion to make him known to those we encounter . . . ? If we look around us, we find people who would be willing to begin—or begin again—a journey of faith were they to encounter Christians in love with Jesus. Shouldn't we and couldn't we be these Christians? I leave you this question: "Am I truly in love with Jesus?

Am I convinced that Jesus offers me and gives me salvation?" And, if I am in love, I have to make him known! But we must be courageous: lay low the mountains of pride and rivalry; fill in the ravines dug by indifference and apathy; make straight the paths of our laziness and our compromises.

May the Virgin Mary . . . help us to tear down the walls and the obstacles that impede our conversion, that is, our journey toward the encounter with the Lord.

*Angelus, December 6, 2015*

## REFLECTION

What obstacles hinder my relationship with Jesus?

## PRAYER

Mother Mary, pray for me that your son Jesus may always find a place in my heart.

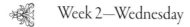 

# God's Kingdom Is Here

Jesus answered, "Those who are well have no need of a physician, but those who are sick; I have come to call not the righteous but sinners to repentance."

—Luke 5:31–32

In the Gospel . . . , John the Baptist's invitation resounds: *"Repent, for the kingdom of heaven is at hand!"* (Mt 3:2) With these very words, Jesus begins his mission in Galilee (cf. Mt 4:17); and such will also be the message that the disciples must bring on their first missionary experience (cf. Mt 10:7). . . . It is a matter of the same joyful message: the kingdom of God is at hand! It is near, and it is in us! These words are very important: "The kingdom of God is in our midst," Jesus says.... This is the central message of every Christian mission. When a missionary goes, [when] a Christian goes to proclaim Jesus . . . he goes simply to proclaim: "The kingdom of God is in our midst!" And in this way, the missionaries prepare the path for Jesus to encounter the people.

*Angelus, December 4, 2016*

## REFLECTION

What does the kingdom of God mean to me?

## PRAYER

Lord, I believe that your kingdom is here, growing in the midst of the world, and that in heaven we will experience it in its fullness. Increase in me the virtue of hope.

# Abandoning Our Idols

No one can say "Jesus is Lord" except by the Holy Spirit.

—1 Corinthians 12:3

The good news that Jesus brings us—and that John [the Baptist] predicts—is that we do not need to wait for the kingdom of God in the future; it is at hand. In some way it is already present and we may experience spiritual power from now on. . . . God comes to establish his lordship in our history, today, every day, in our life; and there—where it is welcomed with faith and humility—love, joy, and peace blossom.

The condition for entering and being a part of this kingdom is to implement a change in our life, which is to *convert*, to convert every day.... It is a question of leaving behind the comfortable but misleading ways of the idols of this world: success at all costs, power to the detriment of the weak, the desire for wealth, pleasure at any price. And instead, preparing the way of the Lord; this does not take away our freedom, but gives us true happiness.

*Angelus, December 4, 2016*

## REFLECTION

What idols do I want to renounce in my life?

## PRAYER

Jesus, I love you and want to give you my whole heart and soul. Help me to always give you the first place in my life.

# The Desert Leads to God

And the Spirit immediately drove him [Jesus] out
into the wilderness.

—Mark 1:12

"Comfort, comfort my people, says your God. Speak
tenderly to Jerusalem, and cry to her that her warfare is ended, that her iniquity is pardoned. . . . 'A voice
cries: In the wilderness prepare the way of the Lord,
make straight in the desert a highway for our God. Every
valley shall be lifted up, and every mountain and hill be
made low; the uneven ground shall become level, and
the rough places a plain. And the glory of the Lord shall
be revealed, and all flesh shall see it together, for the
mouth of the Lord has spoken'" (40:1–2, 3–5).

The Prophet addresses the people who are living the tragedy of the Exile in Babylon, and now instead they hear that they may return to their land, across a path made smooth and wide, without valleys and mountains that make the journey arduous, a level path across the desert. Thus, preparing that path means preparing *a way of salvation and liberation* from every obstacle and hindrance....

*The desert* is a place in which it is difficult to live, but precisely there, one can ... *return not only to the homeland, but return to God, and return to hoping and smiling.* When we are in darkness, in difficulty, we do not smile, and it is precisely hope which teaches us to smile in order to find the path that leads to God.

*General Audience, December 7, 2016*

## REFLECTION

How is God helping me to create a path through the desert of my life?

## PRAYER

Jesus, smooth out the rough places in my life so that I may follow you more closely.

# What the Darkness Can Teach Us

"A voice cries out:
In the wilderness prepare the way of the LORD,
    make straight in the desert a highway for our God.
Every valley shall be lifted up,
    and every mountain and hill be made low. . . . ;
Then the glory of the LORD shall be revealed."

—Isaiah 40:3–5

When we are in darkness . . . it is precisely hope which teaches us to . . . find the path that leads to God. One of the first things that happens to people who distance themselves from God is that they . . . do not smile. . . . Only hope brings a smile: it is the hopeful smile in the expectation of finding God.

Life is often a desert, it is difficult to walk in life, but if we trust in God it can become beautiful and wide as a highway. Just never lose hope, just continue to believe, always, in spite of everything. When we are before a child, although we have many problems and many difficulties, a smile comes to us from within, because we see hope in front of us: a child is hope! And in this way we must be able to discern in life the way of hope which leads us to find God, God who became a child for us. He will make us smile, he will give us everything!

*General Audience, December 7, 2016*

## REFLECTION

What do I hope for during this Advent season?

## PRAYER

Jesus, even in the darkness you give us reason to hope. I thank you for all the good things you have put into my life. Fill me with hope as I look forward to Christmas.

# WEEK 3

# *Mary, Icon of God's Mercy*

---

*A Note for the Third and Fourth Week of Advent*

  *From December 17 to 24, the weekday liturgical texts are arranged by date, not by the day of the week. See page 53 and following for these reflections.*

---

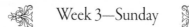 

# Mary Shows Us How We Are Loved

The LORD, your God, is in your midst, . . .
he will rejoice over you with gladness,
   he will renew you in his love;
he will exult over you with loud singing . . .

—Zephaniah 3:17

These words of the prophet Zephaniah, addressed to Israel, may also be referred to our Mother, the Virgin Mary, to the Church, to each one of us, to our souls, all of which God loves with merciful love. Yes, God loves us so much that he even rejoices and takes pleasure in us. He loves us with gratuitous love, limitless love and expects nothing in return. . . .

In Mary, God rejoices and is especially pleased. In one of the prayers dearest to Christians, the *Salve Regina*, we call Mary "Mother of Mercy." She has experienced divine mercy, and has hosted in her womb the very source of this mercy: Jesus Christ. She, who has always lived intimately united to her Son, knows better than anyone what He wants: that all men be saved, and that God's tenderness and consolation never fail anyone. May Mary, Mother of Mercy, help us to understand how much God loves us.

*Homily, December 12, 2015*

## REFLECTION

How would I describe my relationship with Mother Mary? How can I improve it?

## PRAYER

Hail, holy Queen, Mother of Mercy, our life, our sweetness, and our hope . . . turn your eyes of mercy toward us, and after this our exile, show unto us the blessed fruit of your womb, Jesus (From the *Salve Regina*).

# Mary, the First Disciple and Missionary

"And blessed is she who believed that there would be a fulfillment of what was spoken to her by the Lord."

—Luke 1:45

When God comes to encounter us, he moves us inwardly; he sets in motion what we are until our whole life is transformed into praise and blessing. When God visits us, he leaves us restless, with the healthy restlessness of those who feel they have been called to proclaim that he lives and is in the midst of his people. This is what we see in Mary, the first disciple and missionary, the new Ark of the Covenant who, far from remaining in the reserved space of our temples, goes out to visit and accompany the gestation of John with her presence....

Mary is thus the icon of the disciple, of the believing and prayerful woman who is able to accompany and encourage our faith and our hope in the various stages through which we must pass.

*Homily, December 12, 2016*

## REFLECTION

What can I learn from Mary's example of discipleship?

## PRAYER

Mary, you are our spiritual mother, who gently guides us along the path to Christ. Pray for us that we may learn from you how to become more like your son, Jesus.

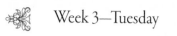 

# Mary, Bearer of Christ and Witness to Love

But God, who is rich in mercy, out of the great love with which he loved us even when we were dead through our trespasses, made us alive together with Christ.

—Ephesians 2:4

In imitation of Mary, we are called to become bearers of Christ and witnesses to his love, looking first of all to those who are privileged in the eyes of Jesus. It is they who he himself indicated: "I was hungry and you gave me food, I was thirsty and you gave me drink, I was a stranger and you welcomed me, I was naked and you clothed me, I was sick and you visited me, I was in prison and you came to me" (Mt 25:35–36).

. . . In our life everything is a gift, it is all mercy. May the Blessed Virgin, first fruit of the saved, model of the Church, Holy and Immaculate Spouse, loved by the Lord, help us to ever increasingly rediscover divine mercy as the distinguishing mark of Christians. One cannot understand a true Christian who is not merciful, just as one cannot comprehend God without his mercy.

*Angelus, December 8, 2015*

## REFLECTION

Do I see everything in my life as a gift of God's mercy?

## PRAYER

God our loving Father, I thank you for sending your Son Jesus to save us from our sins. Deliver us from all evil and guard us with your loving care and protection.

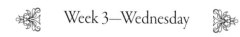
# Mary Carries the Mystery Within

Thanks be to God for his indescribable gift!

—2 Corinthians 9:15

Just after having conceived in faith the Son of God,
[Mary] makes the long trip . . . to visit and help her
cousin Elizabeth. The Angel Gabriel had revealed to
her that her elderly relative, who did not have children,
was in her sixth month of pregnancy (cf. Lk 1:26–36).
That's why Our Lady, who carried within her a gift and
an even greater mystery, goes to see Elizabeth. . . . After
[Mary's] greeting, Elizabeth feels enveloped in great
*astonishment* . . . echoed in these words: "And why is

this granted me, that the mother of my Lord should come to me?" (v. 43) . . .

At Christmas, God gives us all of himself by giving his only Son, who is all his joy. It is only with the heart of Mary, the humble and poor daughter of Zion, who became the Mother of the Son of the Most High, that it is possible to rejoice and be glad for the great gift of God and for his unpredictable surprise.

*Angelus, December 20, 2015*

## REFLECTION

How do I share the gift of Jesus with others?

## PRAYER

Father, open my heart to a spirit of thanksgiving, that I may praise you for all of the incredible gifts of nature and of grace that you have poured out on me.

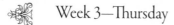 Week 3—Thursday

## Imitating Mary's "Yes"

For the Son of God, Jesus Christ, whom we proclaimed among you . . . was not "Yes and No"; but in him it is always "Yes."

—2 Corinthians 1:19

Mary responds to God's proposal by saying: "Behold, I am the handmaid of the Lord" (v. 38). She does not say: "Well, this time I will do God's will; I will make myself available, then I will see. . . ." No. Hers is a full, total "yes," for her entire life, without conditions. . . . Mary's "yes" opened the path to God among us. It is the most important "yes" in history, the humble "yes" . . . the faithful "yes" that heals disobedience, the willing "yes" that overturns the vanity of sin.

For each of us, too, there is a history of salvation made up of "yeses" and "no's." . . . In this Advent journey, God wishes to visit us and awaits our "yes." . . . With generosity and trust, like Mary, let us say today, each of us, this personal "yes" to God.

*Angelus, December 8, 2016*

## REFLECTION

Where is God asking me to say "Yes" in his plan for my life?

## PRAYER

Father, thank you for inviting me to share your life through Jesus, your Son. Thank you for sending Jesus into the world. Help me to follow him with gladness and joy.

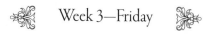
# Mary Gives Flesh to the Gospel

When they saw that the star had stopped, they were
overwhelmed with joy. On entering the house, they
saw the child with Mary his mother.

—Matthew 2:10–11

Celebrating Mary is, first and foremost, remembering our mother, remembering that we are not and
never will be an orphaned people. We have a Mother!
And where there is a mother, there is always the presence
and flavor of home. Where there is a mother, brothers
and sisters may fight, but the sense of unity will always
prevail. Where there is a mother, the struggle for

fraternity will not be lacking. It has always impressed me to see . . . those struggling mothers who, often alone, manage to support their children. This is how Mary is. Mary is this way with us: . . . a woman who fights against the society of distrust and blindness, the society of apathy and dispersion; a woman who fights to strengthen the joy of the Gospel, who fights to give "flesh" to the Gospel.

*Homily, December 12, 2016*

## REFLECTION

How does Mary inspire me to give "flesh" to Jesus?

## PRAYER

Mary my loving mother, you never want to draw attention to yourself. Instead, you always lead us to Jesus. Pray for me that I may grow in a closer loving union with your son.

# WEEK 4

# *Waiting in Hope*

# God Is Close with His Tenderness

And the crowds asked him [John the Baptist], "What then should we do?" In reply he said to them, "Whoever has two coats must share with anyone who has none; and whoever has food must do likewise."

—Luke 3:10–11

We feel that this question—"*What shall we do?*"—is ours. . . . In the words of John, . . . it is necessary to repent, to change direction and take the path of justice, solidarity, sobriety; these are the essential values of a fully human and genuinely Christian life. *Repent*! It sums up the message of the Baptist. . . .

Whoever repents and approaches the Lord, feels joy. . . . Today, it takes courage to speak of joy, which, above all, requires faith! The world is beset by many problems, the future is burdened by uncertainties and fears. Yet, Christians are a joyful people, and their joy is not something superficial and ephemeral, but deep and stable, because it is a gift from the Lord that fills life. Our joy comes from the certainty that "the Lord is at hand" (Phil 4:5); he is close with his tenderness, his mercy, his forgiveness, and his love.

*Angelus, December 13, 2015*

## REFLECTION

Do I reach out to others with joy and hope in spite of my problems and anxieties?

## PRAYER

Saint John the Baptist, you prepared the way for the Lord Jesus. Pray for us that we might prepare for his coming at Christmas by deeds of mercy toward others.

# December 17

## Do We Welcome Him?

God sent his Son, born of a woman, born under the law, in order to redeem those who were under the law, so that we might receive adoption as children.

—Galatians 4:4–5

In a unique way, God drew near to mankind, taking on flesh through a woman. . . .

To us too, in a different way, God draws near with his grace in order to enter our life and offer us the gift of his Son. What do we do? Do we welcome him, let him draw near, or do we reject him, push him away? As Mary, freely offering herself to the Lord of history, allowed him to change the destiny of mankind, so too can we, by welcoming Jesus and seeking to follow him each day, cooperate in his salvific plan for us and for the world. Mary thus appears to us as a model to look to and upon whose support we can count in our search for God, in our closeness to God, in thus allowing God to draw close to us and in our commitment to build the culture of love.

*Angelus, December 18, 2016*

## REFLECTION

When do I feel God drawing near to me?

## PRAYER

Draw close to us, Jesus, and fill us with your grace. Help us to welcome you into our lives and to imitate your examples of love.

 December 18

# God Remembers Us Always

O Israel, trust in the LORD!
You who fear the LORD, trust in the LORD!
The LORD has been mindful of us; he will bless us.

—Psalm 115:9, 11, 12

The Lord always remembers. Even in the bad times he remembers us. And this is our hope. And hope does not disappoint. Never. . . . Idols always disappoint; they are make-believe; they are not real. Here is the wonderful reality of hope: in trusting in the Lord, we become like him. His blessing transforms us into his children who share in his life. Hope in God allows us to enter, so to speak, within the range of his remembrance, of his memory that blesses us and saves us. And it is then that a Hallelujah can burst forth in praise to the living and true God, who was born for us of Mary, died on the Cross and rose again in glory. And in this God we have hope, and this God—who is not an idol—never disappoints.

*General Audience, January 11, 2017*

## REFLECTION

God never forgets us. How has God been present in the various experiences of my life?

## PRAYER

My God, I hope in you. As Christmas draws near, help me to live with a holy anticipation for the joy of your birth.

 December 19

# God Walks with Us

The LORD upholds all who are falling,
and raises up all who are bowed down.

—Psalm 145:14

"The Lord is near," the Apostle Paul tells us, and nothing should perturb us. He is close by.... The greatest mercy lies in his being in our midst, in our being in his presence and company. He walks with us, he shows us the path of love, he lifts us up when we fall and with such tenderness he supports us in our labors; he accompanies us in every circumstance of life. He opens our eyes to see our wretchedness and that of the world, but at the same time he fills us with hope. "The peace of God [ ... ]

will keep your hearts and minds in Christ Jesus" (Phil 4:7), Saint Paul tells us. This is the source of our peaceful and happy life; nothing can deprive us of this peace and joy, despite the suffering and trials of life. The Lord gently opens his heart to us, opens us to his love.

*Homily, December 12, 2015*

## REFLECTION

Jesus' peace is not of this world. When have I been able to feel this peace?

## PRAYER

Jesus, open my heart to your love. I want to love you in return and to spread your love to all whom I meet today.

# Christmas Fulfills Our Hope

Look, the virgin shall conceive and bear a son,
  and they shall name him Emmanuel,"
which means, "God is with us."

—Matthew 1:23

Mary and Joseph, who were the first to welcome Jesus through faith, introduce us to the mystery of Christmas. Mary helps us to assume an attitude of openness in order to welcome the Son of God into our concrete life. . . . Joseph spurs us to always seek God's will and to follow it with full trust. Both allow God to draw near to them.

. . . The angel says: "The child shall be called Emmanuel, which means God-with-us," in other words,

God near to us. And to God who draws near, do I open the door . . . when I hear him ask me to do something more for others, when he calls me to pray?

God-with-us, God who draws near. This message of hope, which is fulfilled at Christmas, leads to fulfillment of the expectation of God in each one of us too, in all the Church, and in the many little ones whom the world scorns, but whom God also loves and to whom God draws near.

*Angelus, December 18, 2016*

## REFLECTION

God is among us. How do I encounter him as I go about my day?

## PRAYER

Mary, you welcomed the Lord with joy when the angel Gabriel came to announce to you the good news of his coming. Pray for me that I may always rejoice in the presence of the Lord who dwells within me through grace.

# December 21

## Christ's Birth Is the Source of Hope

Rejoice in hope, be patient in suffering, persevere in prayer.

—Romans 12:12

When we speak of hope, often it refers to what is not in man's power to realize, which is invisible. In fact, what we hope for goes beyond our strength and our perception. But the birth of Christ, inaugurating redemption, speaks to us of a different hope, a dependable, visible, and understandable hope, because it is founded in God. He comes into the world and gives us the strength to walk with him. . . . Thus, for a Christian, to hope means the certainty of being on a journey with Christ toward the Father who awaits us. Hope is never still; hope is always journeying, and it makes us journey. This hope, which the Child of Bethlehem gives us, offers a destination, a sure, ongoing goal: salvation of mankind, blessedness to those who trust in a merciful God. Saint Paul summarizes all this with the expression: "in this hope we were saved" (Rom 8:24). In other words, walking in this world, with hope, we are saved.

*General Audience, December 21, 2016*

## REFLECTION

Where am I on my journey of hope toward Jesus and God?

## PRAYER

Jesus, the joy of your birth is coming quickly. Help me today not to get so wrapped up in Christmas preparations that I lose my focus on you.

# Christ's Self-Abasement

[Christ Jesus] . . . emptied himself,
   taking the form of a slave,
   being born in human likeness.

—Philippians 2:7

"The Word became flesh" with the intention of sharing all our frailties—with the intention of experiencing our human condition, even unto taking the Cross upon himself, with all the pain of human existence. Such is the depth of his compassion and mercy: self-abasement in order to become a companion at the service of wounded humanity. No sin can erase his merciful closeness or prevent him from outpouring the grace of conversion, provided we invoke it. Indeed, sin itself renders more radiant the love of God who sacrificed his Son to ransom a slave. This mercy of God comes to us with the gift of the Holy Spirit which, in Baptism, enables, generates, and nourishes the new life of his disciples. For, howsoever serious and grave the sins of the world may be, the Spirit, who renews the face of the earth, makes possible the miracle of a life that is more human, more full of joy and hope.

*Homily, December 12, 2015*

## REFLECTION

How does the Holy Spirit encourage me to become more self-sacrificial?

## PRAYER

Jesus, the Word of the Father, you came to Earth and lived among us. I cannot grasp the depth of this mystery, but it reveals your love. Help me to love you in return and to draw others into it.

# Joy at His Coming

I will greatly rejoice in the LORD,
    my whole being shall exult in my God;
for he has clothed me with the garments of salvation,
    he has covered me with the robe of righteousness.

—Isaiah 61:10

We are called to let ourselves be drawn in by the feeling of exultation. . . . A Christian who isn't joyful is a Christian who is lacking something, or else is not a Christian! It is heartfelt joy, the joy within which leads us forth and gives us courage. The Lord comes, he comes into our life as a liberator; he comes to free us from all forms of interior and exterior slavery. It is he who shows us the path of faithfulness, of patience and of perseverance because, upon his return, our joy will be overflowing.

Christmas is near; the signs of his approach are evident along our streets and in our houses. . . . These outward signs invite us to welcome the Lord, who always comes and knocks at our door, knocks at our heart, in order to draw near to us; he invites us to recognize his footsteps among the brothers and sisters who pass beside us, especially the weakest and most needy.

*Angelus, December 11, 2016*

## REFLECTION

As Christmas approaches, how can my joy and excitement be translated into concrete action for the needy?

## PRAYER

Jesus, amid the noise and parties of this season, you gently knock at the door of my heart. I want to listen to your invitation and welcome you with love.

 December 24

# The Taste of True Joy

Rejoice in the Lord always; again I will say, Rejoice. Let your gentleness be known to everyone. The Lord is near.

—Philippians 4:4–5

It is not a superficial or purely emotional cheerfulness that the Apostle exhorts, nor is it the cheerfulness of worldliness or of consumerism. No, it is not that, but rather, it entails a more authentic joy, the taste of which we are called to rediscover. The taste of true joy. It is a joy that touches our innermost being, as we await Jesus, who has already come to bring salvation to the world, the promised Messiah, born in Bethlehem of the Virgin Mary. . . .

God has entered history in order to free us from the slavery of sin; he set his tent in our midst in order to share our existence, to heal our lesions, to bind our wounds and to give us new life. Joy is the fruit of this intervention of God's salvation and love. . . .

*Angelus, December 11, 2016*

## REFLECTION

Can I take several moments throughout the day to thank Jesus for coming into my life?

## PRAYER

Today is Christmas Eve; Advent is almost over. Jesus, even if I don't feel ready for your coming, you invite me to rejoice. You come to offer your grace to all. Help me to receive it with a joyful heart.

## APPENDIX I

# *Today Is Born Our Savior*

# The Power of Love

For a child has been born for us,
  a son given to us;
authority rests upon his shoulders;
  and he is named
Wonderful Counselor, Mighty God,
  Everlasting Father, Prince of Peace.

—Isaiah 9:6

The power of this Child, Son of God and Son of Mary, is not the power of this world, based on might and wealth; it is the power of love. It is the power that created the heavens and the earth, and gives life to all creation: to minerals, plants, and animals. It is the force that attracts man and woman, and makes them one flesh, one single existence. It is the power that gives new birth, forgives sin, reconciles enemies, and transforms evil into good. It is the power of God. This power of love led Jesus Christ to strip himself of his glory and become man; it led him to give his life on the cross and to rise from the dead. It is the power of service, which inaugurates in our world the Kingdom of God, a kingdom of justice and peace. . . .

Dear brothers and sisters,

"For to us a child is born, to us a son is given"; he is the "Prince of peace." Let us welcome him!

*Urbi et Orbi, December 25, 2016*

## REFLECTION

God's love is made present to us today in Jesus, the Christ Child. How shall I adore and worship him?

## PRAYER

Lord Jesus, I rejoice in the mystery of your birth. Though you are the infinite, mighty God, you came among us as an infant. Thank you for the gift of yourself, and help me to give myself wholly to you.

 The Holy Family

# An Authentic School of the Gospel

When they had finished everything required by the law of the Lord, they returned to Galilee, to their own town of Nazareth. The child grew and became strong, filled with wisdom; and the favor of God was upon him.

—Luke 2:39–40

The nuclear family of Jesus, Mary, and Joseph is for each believer and especially for families an authentic school of the Gospel. Here we admire the fulfillment of the divine plan to make of the family a special community of life and love. . . . The classic traits of the Holy Family are: reflection and prayer, mutual understanding and respect, and a spirit of sacrifice, work, and solidarity.

From the exemplary witness of the Holy Family, each family can find precious guidance ... and can draw strength and wisdom for each day's journey. Our Lady and Joseph teach us to welcome children as a gift of God.... It is in a united family that children bring their existence to maturity, living out the meaningful and effective experience of freely given love, tenderness, reciprocal respect, mutual understanding, forgiveness, and joy.

*Angelus, December 27, 2015*


## Reflection

Being a family often challenges us. What are some ways that I can be a witness for family life?


## Prayer

God our loving Father, thank you for the gift of the Holy Family, which teaches us how to make our families places of love. Help us to make our families into true domestic churches, where all find a place at the table of love.

# January 1 — Mary, Mother of God

# We Are Not Orphans

When Jesus saw his mother and the disciple whom he loved standing beside her, he said to his mother, "Woman, here is your son." Then he said to the disciple, "Here is your mother." And from that hour the disciple took her into his own home.

—John 19:26–27

To celebrate Mary as Mother of God and our mother at the beginning of the new year means recalling a certainty that will accompany our days: we are a people with a Mother; we are not orphans. . . .

To begin the year by recalling God's goodness in the maternal face of Mary, in the maternal face of the Church, in the faces of our own mothers, protects us from the corrosive disease of being "spiritual orphans." It is the sense of being orphaned that the soul experiences when it feels motherless and lacking the tenderness of God, when the sense of belonging to a family, a people, a land, to our God, grows dim. . . . Jesus, at the moment of his ultimate self-sacrifice, on the cross, sought to keep nothing for himself, and in handing over his life, he also handed over to us his Mother. He told Mary: Here is your son; here are your children. We too want to receive her into our homes, our families, our communities and nations. We want to meet her maternal gaze.

*Homily, January 1, 2017*

## REFLECTION

We are not alone; we are loved and we have a home. With whom can I share this comforting news?

## PRAYER

Mary, thank you for being our spiritual mother, a gift and a task that you accepted from Jesus on the cross. I want to live under your loving gaze, within your maternal presence. Be with me always. Amen.

# Light Streaming from the Face of Christ

Arise, shine; for your light has come,
  and the glory of the LORD has risen upon you.

—Isaiah 60:1

Ｗe do well to repeat the question asked by the Magi: "Where is the child who has been born the King of the Jews? For we observed his star at its rising, and have come to pay him homage" (Mt 2:2). We are impelled, especially in an age like our own, to seek the signs which God offers us, realizing that great effort is needed to interpret them and thus to understand his will. We are challenged to go to Bethlehem, to find the

Child and his Mother. Let us follow the light which God offers us—that tiny light. . . . The light which streams from the face of Christ, full of mercy and fidelity. And once we have found him, let us worship him with all our heart, and present him with our gifts: our freedom, our understanding, and our love. True wisdom lies concealed in the face of this Child.

*Homily, January 6, 2016*

## REFLECTION

What gifts do I want to offer Jesus?

## PRAYER

Jesus, sometimes the world seems so dark. But you are the light of the world, a light that warms hearts and brings life. Help me to always live in the light of your love.

# APPENDIX II

# *Prayers of Pope Francis*

# 1

# Act of Veneration to the Immaculate Conception at the Spanish Steps

Today the People of God celebrate, they venerate you, the Immaculate, ever preserved from the stain of sin.

Accept the homage I offer you in the name of the Church in Rome and throughout the world.

Knowing that you, our Mother, are totally free from sin is a consolation to us.

Knowing that evil has no power over you fills us with hope and strength in our daily struggle against the threat of the evil one.

But in this struggle we are not alone, we are not orphans, for Jesus, before dying on the Cross, gave you to us as our Mother.

Though we are sinners, we are still your children, the children of the Immaculate, called to that holiness that has shown resplendent in you by the grace of God from the beginning.

Inspired by this hope, today we invoke your motherly protection for us, our families, this city and the world.

Through your intercession, may the power of God's love that preserved you from original sin, free humanity from every form of spiritual and material slavery and make God's plan of salvation victorious in hearts and in history.

May grace prevail over pride in us, too, your children.

May we become merciful as our heavenly Father is merciful.

In this time leading up to the celebration of Jesus' birth, teach us to go against the current: to strip ourselves, to be humble, and giving, to listen and be silent, to go out of ourselves, granting space to the beauty of God, the source of true joy.

Pray for us, our Immaculate Mother!

*December 8, 2014*

# 2

# Prayer in Honor of Mary, Our Immaculate Mother

O Mary, our Immaculate Mother,
  On your feast day I come to you,
And I come not alone:
I bring with me all those with whom your Son
  entrusted to me,
In this city of Rome and in the entire world,
That you may bless them and preserve them
  from harm.
I bring to you, Mother, children,
Especially those who are alone, abandoned,
And for this reason are tricked and exploited.
I bring to you, Mother, families,
Who carry forward life and society
With their daily and hidden efforts;
In a special way the families who struggle the most
For their many internal and external problems.

I bring to you, Mother, all workers, both
    men and women,
And I entrust to you especially those who,
    out of need,
Are forced to work in an unworthy profession
And those who have lost work or are unable
    to find it.
We are in need of your immaculate gaze,
To rediscover the ability to look upon persons
    and things
With respect and awareness,
Without egotistical or hypocritical interests.
We are in need of your immaculate heart,
To love freely,
Without secondary aims but seeking the good
    of the other,
With simplicity and sincerity, renouncing masks
    and tricks.
We are in need of your immaculate hands,
To caress with tenderness,
To touch the flesh of Jesus
In our poor, sick, or despised brethren,
To raise up those who have fallen and support
    those who waver.

We are in need of your immaculate feet,
To go toward those who know not how to make
the first step,
To walk on the paths of those who are lost,
To find those who feel alone.
We thank you, O Mother, because in showing
yourself to us
You free us of all stain of sin;
You remind us that what comes first is the grace
of God,
The love of Jesus Christ who gave his life for us,
The strength of the Holy Spirit which renews
all things.
Let us not give in to discouragement,
But, trusting in your constant help,
Let us engage ourselves fully in renewal of self,
Of this city and of the entire world.
Pray for us, Holy Mother of God!

*December 8, 2016*

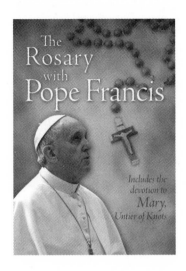

Includes the
devotion to
Mary,
Untier of Knots

## The Rosary with Pope Francis

*Compiled and with an introduction
by Marianne Lorraine Trouvé, FSP*

This book offers the insightful words of Pope Francis for each Hail Mary, using quotes from the Holy Father's various homilies, addresses, and written texts.

Paperback, 112 pages
0-8198-6500-1      978-0-8198-6500-7
$9.95 USD

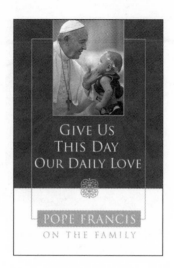

## Give Us This Day Our Daily Love

### Pope Francis on the Family

*Compiled by Theresa Aletheia Noble, FSP
and Donna Giaimo, FSP*

In his direct and delightful style, Pope Francis offers
families a banquet of encouragement; inspiration; and
wise, practical advice.

Paperback, 192 pages
0-8198-3135-2      978-0-8198-3135-4
$12.95 USD

**BOOKS & MEDIA**

A mission of the Daughters of St. Paul

As apostles of Jesus Christ, evangelizing today's world:

We are CALLED to holiness
by God's living Word and Eucharist.

We COMMUNICATE the Gospel message
through our lives and through all
available forms of media.

We SERVE the Church
by responding to the hopes and needs
of all people with the Word of God,
in the spirit of St. Paul.

For more information visit our website:
www.pauline.org.

# *Pauline* BOOKS & MEDIA

The Daughters of St. Paul operate book and media centers at the following addresses. Visit, call, or write the one nearest you today, or find us at www.paulinestore.org.

**CALIFORNIA**
3908 Sepulveda Blvd, Culver City, CA 90230 — 310-397-8676
3250 Middlefield Road, Menlo Park, CA 94025 — 650-369-4230

**FLORIDA**
145 S.W. 107th Avenue, Miami, FL 33174 — 305-559-6715

**HAWAII**
1143 Bishop Street, Honolulu, HI 96813 — 808-521-2731

**ILLINOIS**
172 North Michigan Avenue, Chicago, IL 60601 — 312-346-4228

**LOUISIANA**
4403 Veterans Memorial Blvd, Metairie, LA 70006 — 504-887-7631

**MASSACHUSETTS**
885 Providence Hwy, Dedham, MA 02026 — 781-326-5385

**MISSOURI**
9804 Watson Road, St. Louis, MO 63126 — 314-965-3512

**NEW YORK**
115 E. 29th Street, New York City, NY 10016 — 212-754-1110

**SOUTH CAROLINA**
243 King Street, Charleston, SC 29401 — 843-577-0175

**TEXAS**
No book center; for parish exhibits or outreach evangelization, contact:
210-569-0500, or SanAntonio@paulinemedia.com, or P.O. Box 761416, San Antonio, TX 78245

**VIRGINIA**
1025 King Street, Alexandria, VA 22314 — 703-549-3806

**CANADA**
3022 Dufferin Street, Toronto, ON M6B 3T5 — 416-781-9131